Tucked-Away Treasures

14 PATCHWORK PATTERNS FOR LITTLE QUILTS

Paula Barnes and Mary Ellen Robison
of Red Crinoline Quilts

Martingale®
Create with Confidence

Tucked-Away Treasures: 14 Patchwork Patterns for Little Quilts
© 2022 by Paula Barnes and Mary Ellen Robison

Martingale®
18939 120th Ave NE, Suite 101
Bothell, WA 98011-9511 USA
ShopMartingale.com

Printed in the United States of America
27 26 25 24 23 22   8 7 6 5 4 3 2 1

Library of Congress Cataloging-in-Publication Data is available upon request.

ISBN: 978-1-68356-226-9

MISSION STATEMENT

We empower makers who use fabric and yarn
to make life more enjoyable.

CREDITS

PRESIDENT AND
CHIEF VISIONARY OFFICER
Jennifer Erbe Keltner

CONTENT DIRECTOR
Karen Costello Soltys

TECHNICAL EDITOR
Elizabeth Tisinger Beese

COPY EDITOR
Sheila Chapman Ryan

ILLUSTRATOR
Sandy Loi

DESIGN MANAGER
Adrienne Smitke

PRODUCTION MANAGER
Regina Girard

PHOTOGRAPHERS
Adam Albright
Brent Kane

SPECIAL THANKS
*Photography for this book was taken at
Old Cottonwood in Utica, Nebraska.*

Contents

Introduction

A quilt book is a treasure—a compilation of patterns and pictures you turn to time and again to find your next project, peruse inspiration for color combinations, or to dream about what you'll make "someday." However you use the book, we hope you'll grow fond of these 14 patchwork patterns for small quilts.

We both decorate with many little quilts in our homes, just as you do, so we know just how important it is to adjust the scale and add interesting details to these patterns to pack a big visual punch into each one. You'll find smaller quilts that are perfect for tucking into a vignette in your home decor, using as a table runner or topper, or sprucing up a room as a wall hanging. Regardless of how you choose to use them in your home, their timeless style will be appreciated for years to come.

As business partners since 2005, we have been quilters, friends, and even neighbors (though that's been a while ago and many hundreds of miles back and forth since). Our love for sharing patterns, fabrics, and expertise with fellow quilters keeps us teaching, traveling, and actively supporting our online quilt shop, RedCrinolineQuilts.com. You may recognize a few of the quilts included from our annual club, Red Crinoline Favorites. We've remade several to show you the versatility of the patterns and how fabric choices, placement of lights and darks, and use of interesting border fabrics can create an entirely different look. Paula designs fabrics in partnership with Marcus Brothers Textiles. And since we all know it's all about the fabrics, if you can't find just the right pieces in your stash, you might look to her fabric prints for just the right piece at your local quilt shop.

This is our fourth book, but the first to focus on small quilts. While you may know us for our bed-size quilts and large throws, we also love a pattern you can start and finish in less time. That's what you've got here. We hope you find several places in your home to tuck in these treasures!

~ Paula and Mary Ellen

Tucked-Away Treasures

The mystery of vintage boxes, drawers, and small containers always draws us in.
What treasures might they hold? What discoveries await? The on-point Star blocks are
nestled in the quilt center like treasures in a jewel box. A surrounding cheddar print
adds a pop of color for overall sparkle. Can you imagine this beauty on your wall?

FINISHED QUILT: 34" × 34" | FINISHED BLOCK: 6" × 6"

MATERIALS

Yardage is based on 42"-wide fabric.

- ½ yard of light blue print for blocks and inner border
- ½ yard of cheddar print for blocks, setting triangles, and corner triangles
- 1¼ yards of dark blue print for blocks, setting squares, outer border, and binding
- ⅛ yard of green print for blocks
- 1⅛ yards of fabric for backing
- 38" × 38" piece of batting

CUTTING

All measurements include ¼" seam allowances.

From the light blue print, cut:

1 strip, 3½" × 42"; crosscut into 9 squares, 3½" × 3½"
3 strips, 2½" × 42"; crosscut into 36 squares, 2½" × 2½"
4 strips, 1½" × 42"; crosscut into:
    2 strips, 1½" × 28"
    2 strips, 1½" × 26"

From the cheddar print, cut:

2 squares, 9¾" × 9¾"; cut into quarters diagonally to yield 8 setting triangles
2 squares, 5⅛" × 5⅛"; cut in half diagonally to yield 4 corner triangles
1 strip, 3½" × 42"; crosscut into 9 squares, 3½" × 3½"

From the dark blue print, cut:

1 strip, 6½" × 42"; crosscut into 4 squares, 6½" × 6½"
4 strips, 3½" × 42"; crosscut into:
    2 strips, 3½" × 34"
    2 strips, 3½" × 28"
2 strips, 3½" × 42"; crosscut into 18 squares, 3½" × 3½"
4 strips, 2" × 42"

From the green print, cut:

1 strip, 2½" × 42"; crosscut into 9 squares, 2½" × 2½"

Trimming Hourglass Units

We like to make hourglass units oversized and trim them after sewing. This guarantees that the units will be the exact size needed.

1. Place a square ruler on top of the unit, aligning the 45° line of the ruler with the diagonal seam line of the hourglass unit. Divide the desired trimmed size of the block by two and make sure those lines of the ruler meet at the center of the block. For the 2½" unfinished units, place the 1¼" lines at the center of the unit. The 2½" lines of the ruler should line up with the opposite diagonal seam of the hourglass unit.

2. Trim the unit along the top and right edges of the ruler.

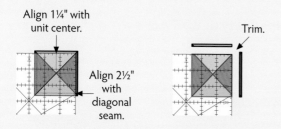

Align 1¼" with unit center.

Align 2½" with diagonal seam.

Trim.

3. Rotate the unit so that the newly trimmed sides align with the 2½" lines of the ruler and the 45° line of the ruler is aligned with the diagonal seam line of the hourglass unit. The 1¼" lines should meet in the center of the block as in step 1.

4. Trim the unit along the top and right edges of the ruler. You now have a perfect hourglass unit.

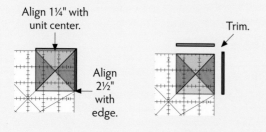

Align 1¼" with unit center.

Align 2½" with edge.

Trim.

MAKING THE BLOCKS

Press the seam allowances as indicated by the arrows in the illustrations.

1. With a pencil, draw two diagonal lines from corner to corner on the wrong side of each light blue 3½" square and cheddar print 3½" square, making an X.

Mark.

2. Place a marked light blue and a dark blue 3½" square right sides together. Sew ¼" from both sides of *one* of the pencil lines. Cut on *both* pencil lines and press to make four units. Repeat to make 36 identical units.

Make 36 units.

3. Repeat step 2 with a marked cheddar and a dark blue 3½" square to make four units. Repeat to make 36 identical units.

Make 36 units.

4. Sew a unit from step 2 to a unit from step 3 to create an hourglass unit. Make 36 identical units. Refer to "Trimming Hourglass Units" on page 8 to trim the units to 2½" square.

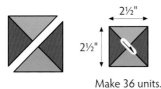

Make 36 units.

5. Arrange and sew four hourglass units, four light blue 2½" squares, and one green 2½" square together into three rows as shown. Sew the rows together to make an

Ohio Star block that measures 6½" square, including seam allowances. Repeat to make nine blocks.

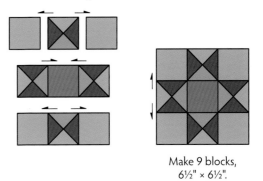

Make 9 blocks,
6½" × 6½".

ASSEMBLING THE QUILT TOP

1. Referring to the quilt assembly diagram below, arrange and sew the blocks and dark blue 6½" squares together in diagonal rows, adding the cheddar setting triangles to the ends of each row as indicated. Join the rows, adding the cheddar corner triangles last. The quilt top should measure 26" square, including seam allowances.

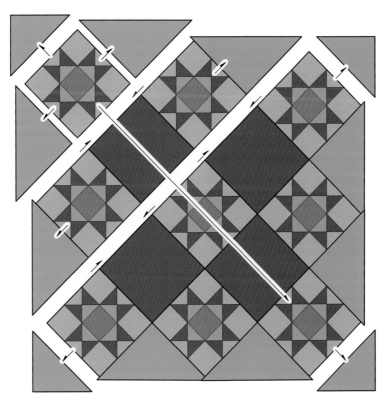

Quilt assembly

Designed by Paula Barnes; pieced by Mary Ellen Robison; quilted by Pat Meeks

2. Sew the light blue 1½" × 26" strips to the sides of the quilt. Sew the light blue 1½" × 28" strips to the top and bottom. The quilt top should measure 28" square, including seam allowances.

3. Sew the dark blue 3½" × 28" strips to the sides of the quilt. Sew the dark blue 3½" × 34" strips to the top and bottom. The quilt top should be 34" square.

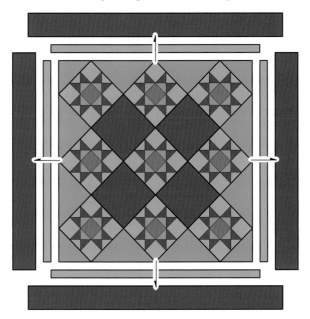

Adding the borders

FINISHING THE QUILT

For more details on any finishing steps, visit ShopMartingale.com/HowtoQuilt for free downloadable information.

1. Layer the quilt top with batting and backing; baste the layers together.

2. Quilt by hand or machine. The quilt shown is machine quilted with an allover meander pattern.

3. Make double-fold binding using the dark blue 2"-wide strips. Attach the binding to the quilt.

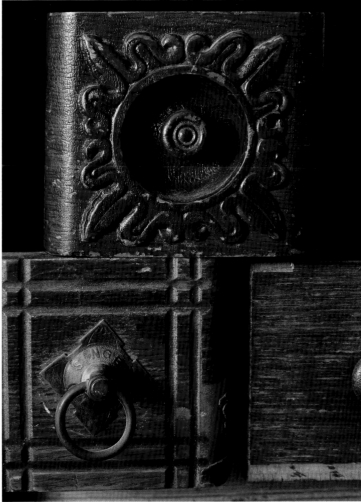

Bountiful Baskets

Spring, summer, fall, and winter—we're here for baskets all year through. Whether they're flower baskets, fruit baskets, or holiday baskets, they're always in season for quilters. A touch of whimsy finishes this dainty mini with pieced borders on just two ends for a quilt that will be equally at home on a wall or tabletop.

FINISHED QUILT: 16½" × 20½" | **FINISHED BLOCK: 5" × 5"**

Designed by Paula Barnes; pieced by Mary Ellen Robison; quilted by Pat Meeks

MATERIALS

Yardage is based on 42"-wide fabric.

- ⅓ yard of beige print for blocks and sashing
- ⅛ yard of bright green print for blocks and sashing
- ⅓ yard of red print for blocks, sashing, and sawtooth border
- ½ yard of dark green print for blocks, border, sawtooth border, and binding
- ⅝ yard of fabric for backing
- 21" × 25" piece of batting
- 1" finished Star Singles papers (optional)*

*See "Using Star Singles" on page 14 before cutting fabrics.

CUTTING

All measurements include ¼" seam allowances.

From the beige print, cut:
2 strips, 3¼" × 42"; crosscut into:
    2 squares, 3¼" × 3¼"
    26 squares, 2¼" × 2¼"
2 strips, 1½" × 42"; crosscut into:
    4 strips, 1½" × 5½"
    8 strips, 1½" × 3½"
    4 squares, 1½" × 1½"

From the bright green print, cut:
1 strip, 2¼" × 42"; crosscut into 12 squares, 2¼" × 2¼"
1 strip, 1½" × 42"; crosscut into 13 squares, 1½" × 1½"

Continued on page 14

Continued from page 13

From the red print, cut:

1 strip, 3¼" × 42"; crosscut into 8 squares, 3¼" × 3¼"

1 strip, 2¼" × 42"; crosscut into 10 squares, 2¼" × 2¼"

2 strips, 1½" × 42"; crosscut into 8 strips, 1½" × 5½"

From the dark green print, cut:

1 strip, 3¼" × 42"; crosscut into 10 squares, 3¼" × 3¼"

1 strip, 2¼" × 42"; crosscut into 4 squares, 2¼" × 2¼"

4 strips, 2" × 42"; crosscut *2 of the strips* into:

    2 strips, 2" × 16½"

    2 strips, 2" × 13½"

◆ *Using Star Singles*

If you use 1" finished Star Singles papers, *do not* cut the 2¼" squares from the beige, bright green, red, and dark green prints. Instead, cut the pieces listed below. Then skip steps 1 and 2 of "Making the Blocks" below and follow the package instructions to piece 24 bright green, 8 dark green, and 20 red half-square-triangle units.

From the beige print, cut:

7 squares, 4½" × 4½"

From the bright green print, cut:

3 squares, 4½" × 4½"

From the red print, cut:

3 squares, 4½" × 4½"

From the dark green print, cut:

1 square, 4½" × 4½"

MAKING THE BLOCKS

Press the seam allowances as indicated by the arrows in the illustrations.

1. Referring to "Half-Square-Triangle Units" on page 78, mark the beige 2¼" squares. Layer 12 of the marked squares right sides together with the bright green 2¼" squares. Sew, cut, and press; then trim the units to 1½" square. Make 24 beige/bright green small half-square-triangle units.

Make 24 units.

2. Repeat step 1 with the remaining marked beige, red, and dark green 2¼" squares to make 20 beige/red small half-square-triangle units and eight beige/dark green small half-square-triangle units.

Make 20 units.   Make 8 units.

3. Mark the beige 3¼" squares and layer them right sides together with the dark green 3¼" squares. Sew, cut, and press; then trim the units to 2½" square. Make four large half-square-triangle units.

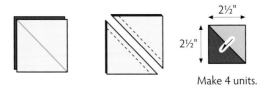

Make 4 units.

4. Sew one beige 1½" square, four beige/bright green small half-square-triangle units, and three beige/red small half-square-triangle units together into two rows as shown. Sew the rows together to create a unit that measures 2½" × 4½", including seam allowances. Make four units.

Make 4 units,
2½" × 4½".

5. Sew two beige/bright green and two beige/red small half-square-triangle units together into two rows as shown. Sew the rows together to create a unit that measures 2½" square, including seam allowances. Make four units.

Make 4 units,
2½" × 2½".

7. Sew a beige/dark green small half-square-triangle unit to the bottom of a beige 1½" × 3½" strip as shown. Make four foot units, each 1½" × 4½", including seam allowances. Repeat to make four reversed foot units.

Make 4 of each unit,
1½" × 4½".

6. Arrange one of each unit from steps 4 and 5 with a large half-square-triangle unit from step 3 as shown. Sew the units into rows and then sew the rows together to complete a basket top. Make four basket tops, each 4½" square, including seam allowances.

Make 4 units,
4½" × 4½".

8. Arrange and sew a basket top from step 6, one foot unit and one reversed foot unit from step 7, and one bright green 1½" square together into two rows. Sew the rows together and press to create a Basket block that measures 5½" square, including seam allowances. Make four blocks.

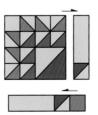

Make 4 blocks,
5½" × 5½".

ASSEMBLING THE QUILT TOP

1. Referring to the quilt assembly diagram, arrange and sew the blocks, red and beige 1½" × 5½" strips, and bright green 1½" squares together into five rows. Note the rotation of the blocks. Sew the rows together to complete the quilt center. The quilt center should measure 13½" square, including seam allowances.

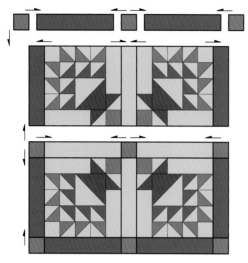

Quilt assembly

2. Sew the dark green 2" × 13½" strips to the sides of the quilt. Sew the dark green 2" × 16½" strips to the top and bottom. The quilt top should measure 16½" square, including seam allowances.

3. To make the sawtooth border, mark the red 3¼" squares and layer them right sides together with the remaining dark green 3¼" squares. Sew, cut, and press; then trim the units to 2½" square. Make 16 half-square-triangle units.

Make 16 units.

4. Join eight half-square-triangle units (four units pointing in one direction and four units pointing in the opposite direction) to make a top border measuring 2½" × 16½", including seam allowances. Repeat to make a bottom border.

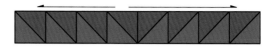

Make 2 borders, 2½" × 16½".

5. Sew the sawtooth borders to the top and bottom edges of the quilt top. The quilt top should measure 16½" × 20½".

Adding the borders

FINISHING THE QUILT

For more details on any finishing steps, visit ShopMartingale.com/HowtoQuilt for free downloadable information.

1. Layer the quilt top with batting and backing; baste the layers together.

2. Quilt by hand or machine. The quilt shown is machine quilted with an allover meander in taupe thread.

3. Make double-fold binding using the remaining dark green 2"-wide strips. Attach the binding to the quilt.

Checkered Stars

The color brown is often associated with solid, dependable traits—sincere and genuine. It's no wonder, then, that a rich brown fabric and the wood tones of vintage cabinets evoke thoughts of security and stability. Mixed with the importance and confidence of navy blue, Checkered Stars and Pinwheels twirl across the quilt top with classic elegance.

FINISHED QUILT: 37½" × 37½" | **FINISHED BLOCK: 6" × 6"**

MATERIALS

Yardage is based on 42"-wide fabric.

- ⅛ yard of tan print for blocks
- ⅓ yard of dark brown print for blocks
- ¾ yard of navy print for blocks, setting triangles, and corner triangles
- ¼ yard of light brown print for blocks
- ⅝ yard of light print for blocks and inner border
- 1 yard of dark brown dot for outer border and binding
- 2⅓ yards of fabric for backing*
- 42" × 42" piece of batting
- 1½" finished Star Singles papers (optional)**

If your backing fabric is 42" wide after prewashing and trimming selvages, you'll only need 1¼ yards.

**See "Using Star Singles" on page 19 before cutting fabrics.*

CUTTING

All measurements include ¼" seam allowances.

From the tan print, cut:
2 strips, 1½" × 42"; crosscut into 4 strips, 1½" × 15"

From the dark brown print, cut:
1 strip, 2¾" × 42"; crosscut into 8 squares, 2¾" × 2¾"
3 strips, 1½" × 42"; crosscut into 5 strips, 1½" × 15"

From the navy print, cut:
1 strip, 9¾" × 42"; crosscut into:
    2 squares, 9¾" × 9¾"; cut into quarters diagonally to yield 8 setting triangles
    2 squares, 5⅛" × 5⅛"; cut in half diagonally to yield 4 corner triangles
1 strip, 2¾" × 42"; crosscut into 8 squares, 2¾" × 2¾"
6 strips, 2" × 42"; crosscut into:
    16 pieces, 2" × 3½"
    72 squares, 2" × 2"

Continued on page 19

Continued from page 17

From the light brown print, cut:

2 strips, 2¾" × 42"; crosscut into 16 squares, 2¾" × 2¾"

From the light print, cut:

7 strips, 2" × 42"; crosscut into:

　36 pieces, 2" × 3½"

　68 squares, 2" × 2"

4 strips, 1¼" × 42"; crosscut into:

　2 strips, 1¼" × 27½"

　2 strips, 1¼" × 26"

From the dark brown dot, cut:

4 strips, 5½" × 42"; crosscut into:

　2 strips, 5½" × 37½"

　2 strips, 5½" × 27½"

5 strips, 2" × 42"

◆ *Using Star Singles*

If you use the 1½" Star Singles papers, *do not* cut the 2¾" squares from the dark brown, navy, and light brown prints. Instead, cut the pieces listed below. Then skip steps 1 and 2 of "Making the Pinwheel Blocks" on page 20 and follow the package instructions to piece 16 navy and 16 dark brown half-square-triangle units.

From the dark brown print, cut:

2 squares, 5½" × 5½"

From the navy print, cut:

2 squares, 5½" × 5½"

From the light brown print, cut:

4 squares, 5½" × 5½"

MAKING THE STAR BLOCKS

Press the seam allowances as indicated by the arrows in the illustrations.

1. Sew one tan and two dark brown 1½" × 15" strips together to make a strip set. Make two strip sets. Crosscut into 18 segments that measure 1½" wide.

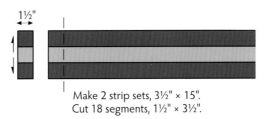

Make 2 strip sets, 3½" × 15".
Cut 18 segments, 1½" × 3½".

2. Sew one dark brown and two tan 1½" × 15" strips together to make a strip set. Crosscut into nine segments, 1½" wide.

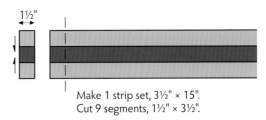

Make 1 strip set, 3½" × 15".
Cut 9 segments, 1½" × 3½".

3. Sew two segments from step 1 together with a segment from step 2 to create a nine-patch unit that measures 3½" square, including seam allowances. Make nine units.

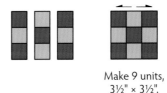

Make 9 units,
3½" × 3½".

4. Draw a diagonal line from corner to corner on the wrong side of the navy 2" squares. Place a marked square on one end of a light 2" × 3½" piece, right sides together. Sew on the marked line. Trim the excess corner fabric ¼" from the stitched line. Place a marked square on the opposite end of the light 2" × 3½" piece. Sew and trim as before to make a flying-geese unit measuring 2" × 3½", including seam allowances. Make 36 units.

Make 36 units,
2" × 3½".

5. Arrange and sew four light 2" squares, four flying-geese units, and one nine-patch unit together into three rows as shown. Sew the rows together to make a block that measures 6½" square, including seam allowances. Make a total of nine Checkered Star blocks.

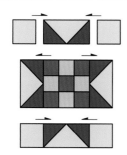 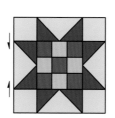

Make 9 blocks,
6½" × 6½".

MAKING THE PINWHEEL BLOCKS

1. Referring to "Half-Square-Triangle Units" on page 78, mark the light brown 2¾" squares. Layer eight of the marked light brown squares right sides together with the navy 2¾" squares. Sew, cut, and press; then trim the units to 2" square. Make 16 light brown/navy half-square-triangle units.

Make 16 units.

2. Using the remaining marked light brown squares and the dark brown 2¾" squares, repeat step 1 to make 16 light brown/dark brown half-square-triangle units.

Make 16 units.

3. Arrange and sew four half-square-triangle units from step 1 together in two rows as shown. Join the rows to make a pinwheel unit. The unit should measure 3½" square, including seam allowances. Make four pinwheel units.

Make 4 units,
3½" × 3½".

4. Draw a diagonal line from corner to corner on the wrong side of the remaining light 2" squares. Place a marked square on one end of a navy 2" × 3½" piece, right sides together. Sew on the marked line. Trim the excess corner fabric ¼" from the stitched line. Place a marked square on the opposite end of the navy 2" × 3½" piece. Sew and trim as before to make a flying-geese unit measuring 2" × 3½", including seam allowances. Make 16 units.

Make 16 units,
2" × 3½".

Designed by Paula Barnes; pieced by Mary Ellen Robison; quilted by Pat Meeks

5. Arrange and sew four half-square-triangle units from step 2, four flying-geese units from step 4, and one pinwheel unit from step 3 together into three rows as shown. Sew the rows together to make a block that measures 6½" square, including seam allowances. Make a total of four Pinwheel blocks.

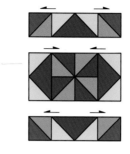 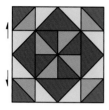

Make 4 blocks,
6½" × 6½".

ASSEMBLING THE QUILT TOP

1. Referring to the quilt assembly diagram below, arrange and sew the Star and Pinwheel blocks together in diagonal rows, adding the navy setting triangles to the ends of each row as indicated. Join the rows, adding the navy corner triangles last. The quilt center should measure 26" square, including seam allowances.

2. Sew the light 1¼" × 26" strips to the sides of the quilt. Sew the light 1¼" × 27½" strips to the top and bottom. The quilt top should measure 27½" square, including seam allowances.

Quilt assembly

3. Sew the dark brown dot 5½" × 27½" strips to the sides of the quilt. Sew the dark brown dot 5½" × 37½" strips to the top and bottom to complete the quilt top, which should measure 37½" square.

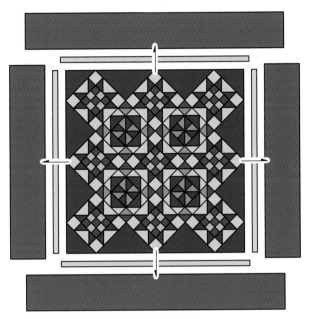

Adding the borders

FINISHING THE QUILT

For more details on any finishing steps, visit ShopMartingale.com/HowtoQuilt for free downloadable information.

1. Layer the quilt top with batting and backing; baste the layers together.

2. Quilt by hand or machine. The quilt shown is machine quilted with an allover meander design.

3. Make double-fold binding using the dark brown dot 2"-wide strips. Attach the binding to the quilt.

Threads of Time

One of the many small satisfactions of quilting is finishing off a spool of thread. There's a little thrill in using it up and thinking of all the stitches that were made with it. So, too, is the excitement of piecing a mini spool from favorite fabrics, then another, and another. At last, you'll have a quilt of patchwork spools aplenty, and your time well spent.

FINISHED QUILT: 30½" × 30½" | FINISHED BLOCK: 3" × 3"

Designed by Paula Barnes; pieced by Mary Ellen Robison; quilted by Cathy Peters and Lynn Graham

MATERIALS

Yardage is based on 42"-wide fabric.

- 4" × 11" piece *each* of 18 assorted light prints for blocks
- 6" × 11" piece *each* of 18 assorted dark prints for blocks
- ⅛ yard *each* of 4 assorted dark blue prints for inner border
- ⅝ yard of black solid for outer border and binding
- 1 yard of fabric for backing
- 35" × 35" piece of batting

CUTTING

All measurements include ¼" seam allowances.

From *each* of the assorted light prints, cut:
2 strips, 1½" × 11"; crosscut into 6 pieces, 1½" × 3½" (108 total; 2 will be extra)

From *each* of the assorted dark prints, cut:
3 strips, 1½" × 11"; crosscut into:
  3 pieces, 1½" × 3½" (54 total; 1 will be extra)
  12 squares, 1½" × 1½" (216 total; 4 will be extra)

From *each* of the assorted dark blue prints, cut:
1 strip, 3½" × 21½" (4 total)

From the black solid, cut:
8 strips, 2" × 42"; crosscut *4 of the strips* into:
  2 strips, 2" × 30½"
  2 strips, 2" × 27½"

MAKING THE BLOCKS

The instructions are for making three blocks at a time. Repeat to piece 18 sets of three matching blocks (54 blocks total; 1 will be extra). Press the seam allowances as indicated by the arrows in the illustrations.

1. Select all pieces cut from one light print and one dark print. Draw a diagonal line from corner to corner on the wrong side of the dark 1½" squares. Place a marked square on each end of a light 1½" × 3½" piece,

right sides together. Sew on the marked lines. Trim the excess corner fabric ¼" from the stitched lines. Make six matching units, each 1½" × 3½", including seam allowances.

Make 6 units,
1½" × 3½".

2. Sew together two units from step 1 with a dark 1½" × 3½" piece as shown to make a Spool block measuring 3½" square, including seam allowances. Make three matching Spool blocks.

Make 3 blocks,
3½" × 3½".

ASSEMBLING THE QUILT TOP

1. Arrange the blocks into seven rows of seven blocks each, rotating the blocks as shown. Sew the blocks into rows and then sew the rows together. The quilt center should measure 21½" square, including seam allowances.

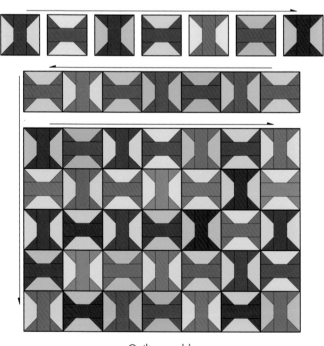

Quilt assembly

2. Sew a dark blue 3½" × 21½" strip to the left and right sides of the quilt. Sew a Spool block to each end of each remaining dark blue 3½" × 21½" strip. Sew these strips to the top and bottom of the quilt. The quilt top should measure 27½" square, including seam allowances.

3. Sew the black 2" × 27½" strips to the sides of the quilt. Sew the black 2" × 30½" strips to the top and bottom to complete the quilt top, which should measure 30½" square.

FINISHING THE QUILT

For more details on any finishing steps, visit ShopMartingale.com/HowtoQuilt for free downloadable information.

1. Layer the quilt top with batting and backing; baste the layers together.

2. Quilt by hand or machine. The quilt shown is machine quilted with an overall spiral design in the quilt center. The borders feature feathers and pearls.

3. Make double-fold binding using the remaining black solid 2"-wide strips. Attach the binding to the quilt.

Adding the borders

Fresh Picked

A mélange of reds in cranberry, cherry, and apple shades is the perfect pick to create a striking little Bear's Paw quilt. If reds aren't a part of your decor, find inspiration in another nature-inspired palette of earthy greens or blues that reflect the sky and water. Make it your own!

FINISHED QUILT: 34" × 34" | **FINISHED BLOCK: 7" × 7"**

MATERIALS

Yardage is based on 42"-wide fabric. Fat quarters are 18" × 21". Fat eighths are 9" × 21".

- 6 fat quarters of assorted light prints for blocks and sashing
- 8 fat eighths of assorted red prints for blocks and sashing
- ⅞ yard of red-and-black print for blocks, outer border, and binding
- ⅛ yard of red floral for sashing squares
- ¼ yard of black print for inner border
- 1⅛ yards of fabric for backing
- 38" × 38" piece of batting
- 1" finished Star Singles papers (optional)*

*See "Using Star Singles" on page 30 before cutting fabrics.

CUTTING

All measurements include ¼" seam allowances.

From *each* of the assorted light prints, cut:
1 strip, 2½" × 21"; crosscut into 2 strips, 2½" × 7½" (12 total)
2 strips, 2¼" × 21"; crosscut into 12 squares, 2¼" × 2¼" (72 total)
2 strips, 1½" × 21"; crosscut into:
  8 pieces, 1½" × 3½" (48 total; 12 will be extra)
  6 squares, 1½" × 1½" (36 total)

From *each* of the assorted red prints, cut:
1 strip, 2½" × 21"; crosscut into 4 squares, 2½" × 2½" (32 total)
1 strip, 2¼" × 21"; crosscut into 9 squares, 2¼" × 2¼" (72 total)
1 strip, 1½" × 21"; crosscut into 6 squares, 1½" × 1½" (48 total; 7 will be extra)

Continued on page 30

Continued from page 29

From the red-and-black print, cut:

4 strips, 4" × 42"; crosscut into:

    2 strips, 4" × 34"

    2 strips, 4" × 27"

1 strip, 2½" × 42"; crosscut into 4 squares, 2½" × 2½"

4 strips, 2" × 42"

From the red floral, cut:

4 squares, 2½" × 2½"

From the black print, cut:

4 strips, 1¼" × 42"; crosscut into:

    2 strips, 1¼" × 27"

    2 strips, 1¼" × 25½"

◆ *Using Star Singles*

If you use the 1" Star Singles papers, *do not* cut the 2¼" squares from the light and red prints. Instead, cut the pieces listed below. Then skip step 1 of "Making the Blocks" below and follow the package instructions to piece 144 red/cream half-square-triangle units.

From *each* of the assorted light prints, cut:

3 squares, 4½" × 4½" (18 total)

From *each* of 2 red prints, cut:

3 squares, 4½" × 4½" (6 total)

From *each* of 6 remaining red prints, cut:

2 squares, 4½" × 4½" (12 total)

MAKING THE BLOCKS

Press the seam allowances as indicated by the arrows in the illustrations. The red print and red-and-black print 2½" squares will be collectively referred to as "red."

1. Referring to "Half-Square-Triangle Units" on page 78, mark the light 2¼" squares and layer them

right sides together with the red 2¼" squares. Sew, cut, and press; then trim the units to 1½" square. Make a total of 144 half-square-triangle units.

Make 144 units.

2. Arrange and sew one light 1½" square, four units from step 1, and one red 2½" square in rows. Sew the rows together to create a unit that measures 3½" square, including seam allowances. Make a total of 36 units, mixing and matching fabrics to make them as scrappy as possible.

Make 36 units,
3½" × 3½".

3. Arrange and sew four units that have matching large red squares, four matching light 1½" × 3½" pieces, and one red 1½" square together in rows. Sew the rows together to make a block that measures 7½" square, including seam allowances. Make a total of nine Bear's Paw blocks.

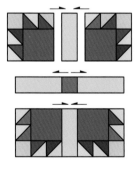 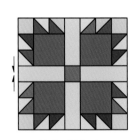

Make 9 blocks,
7½" × 7½".

MAKING THE SASHING UNITS

1. Draw a diagonal line from corner to corner on the wrong side of the remaining red 1½" squares. Place a

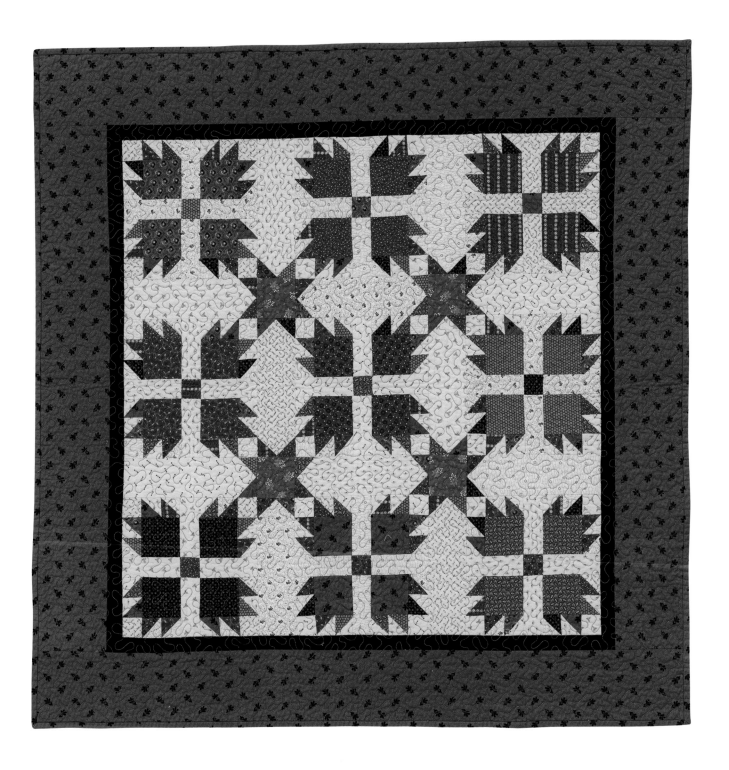

Designed by Paula Barnes; pieced by Mary Ellen Robison; quilted by Pat Meeks

marked square on one corner of a light 2½" × 7½" piece, right sides together. Sew on the marked line. Trim the excess corner fabric ¼" from the stitched line. Place a marked square on an adjacent corner of the light 2½" × 7½" piece. Sew and trim as before to make an outer sashing unit measuring 2½" × 7½", including seam allowances. Make eight outer sashing units.

Make 8 units,
2½" × 7½".

2. In the same manner, add a remaining marked red square to all four corners of the remaining light

2½" × 7½" pieces to make four inner sashing units measuring 2½" × 7½", including seam allowances.

Make 4 units,
2½" × 7½".

ASSEMBLING THE QUILT TOP

1. Arrange the blocks, outer sashing units, inner sashing units, and red floral 2½" sashing squares into rows as shown. Sew the blocks and sashing into three block rows and then sew the sashing pieces and sashing squares into two sashing rows. Join the rows to make the quilt center measuring 25½" square, including seam allowances.

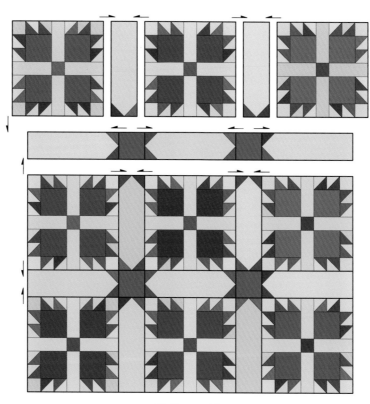

Quilt assembly

2. Sew the black 1¼" × 25½" strips to the sides of the quilt. Sew the black 1¼" × 27" strips to the top and bottom. The quilt top should measure 27" square, including seam allowances.

3. Sew the red-and-black 4" × 27" strips to the sides of the quilt. Sew the red-and-black 4" × 34" strips to the top and bottom to complete the quilt top, which should measure 34" square.

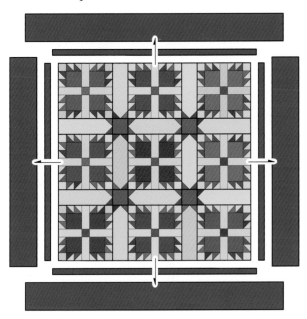

Adding the borders

FINISHING THE QUILT

For more details on any finishing steps, visit ShopMartingale.com/HowtoQuilt for free downloadable information.

1. Layer the quilt top with batting and backing; baste the layers together.

2. Quilt by hand or machine. The quilt shown is machine quilted with an allover meander design.

3. Make double-fold binding using the red-and-black 2"-wide strips. Attach the binding to the quilt.

Fancy That

What is it you fancy? Beautiful architectural details? Rich textures? Conversation with friends over a cup of coffee or tea? Time well spent in your sewing room? All of the above? Us, too. Half-square triangles are elevated to new heights in a blur of Pinwheels and a bursting border. Want to know the secret? Star Singles make sewing triangles a breeze!

FINISHED QUILT: 48½" × 48½" | **FINISHED BLOCK: 3" × 3"**

MATERIALS

Yardage is based on 42"-wide fabric.

- 1⅓ yards of light print for blocks and border #4
- ¼ yard *each* of 5 assorted lavender and tan prints for blocks and border #4 (referred to collectively as "dark")*
- ½ yard of black print for borders #1 and #3
- ½ yard of tan floral for border #2
- ⅜ yard of black solid for binding
- 3⅛ yards of fabric for backing
- 55" × 55" piece of batting
- 3" finished Star Singles papers (optional)**

You can also use fat quarters, which measure 18" × 21".

**See "Using Star Singles" on page 36 before cutting fabrics.*

CUTTING

All measurements include ¼" seam allowances.

From the light print, cut:
9 strips, 4¼" × 42"; crosscut into 80 squares, 4¼" × 4¼"
1 strip, 3½" × 42"; crosscut into 4 squares, 3½" × 3½"

From *each* of the assorted dark prints, cut:
2 strips, 4¼" × 42"; crosscut into 16 squares, 4¼" × 4¼" (80 total)

From the black print, cut:
5 strips, 2" × 42"
4 strips, 1½" × 42"; crosscut into:
    2 strips, 1½" × 32½"
    2 strips, 1½" × 30½"

From the tan floral, cut:
4 strips, 4" × 42"; crosscut into:
    2 strips, 4" × 39½"
    2 strips, 4" × 32½"

From the black solid, cut:
6 strips, 2" × 42"

♦ *Using Star Singles*

If you use the 3" Star Singles papers, *do not* cut the 4¼" squares from the light and dark prints. Instead, cut the pieces listed below. Then skip "Making the Half-Square-Triangle Units" below and follow the package instructions to piece 160 half-square-triangle units.

From the light print, cut:
20 squares, 8½" × 8½"

From *each* of the assorted dark prints, cut:
4 squares, 8½" × 8½" (20 total)

MAKING THE HALF-SQUARE-TRIANGLE UNITS

Press the seam allowances as indicated by the arrows in the illustrations. Referring to "Half-Square-Triangle Units" on page 78, mark the light 4¼" squares and layer them right sides together with the dark 4¼" squares. Sew, cut, and press; then trim the units to 3½" square. Make 160 half-square-triangle units.

3½"

3½"

Make 160 units.

ASSEMBLING THE QUILT TOP

Arrange 100 of the half-square-triangle units into 10 rows of 10 each, rotating each unit as shown. Sew the units into rows and then sew the rows together. The quilt center should measure 30½" square, including seam allowances. Set aside the remaining 60 half-square-triangle units for border #4.

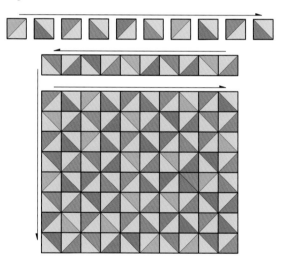

Quilt assembly

ADDING THE BORDERS

1. Referring to the illustration on page 38, sew the black print 1½" × 30½" strips to the sides of the quilt. Sew the black print 1½" × 32½" strips to the top and bottom. The quilt top should measure 32½" square, including seam allowances.

Designed by Paula Barnes; pieced by Mary Ellen Robison; quilted by Pat Meeks

2. Sew the tan floral 4" × 32½" strips to the sides of the quilt. Sew the tan floral 4" × 39½" strips to the top and bottom. The quilt top should measure 39½" square, including seam allowances.

3. Join the black print 2" × 42" strips end to end. From the pieced strip, cut two 42½"-long strips and two 39½"-long strips. Sew the shorter strips to opposite sides of the quilt. Sew the longer strips to the top and bottom edges. The quilt top should measure 42½" square, including seam allowances.

4. Join 14 half-square-triangle units, with seven units pointing in one direction and seven units pointing in the opposite direction, to make a border measuring 3½" × 42½", including seam allowances. Make four. You will have four half-square-triangle units left over.

Make 4 borders, 3½" × 42½".

5. Sew a light print 3½" square to each end of a border from step 4 to make a border measuring 3½" × 48½", including seam allowances. Make two.

Make 2 borders, 3½" × 48½".

6. Sew the shorter triangle borders to the side edges of the quilt top. Sew the longer borders to the top and bottom edges. The quilt top should measure 48½" square.

FINISHING THE QUILT

For more details on any finishing steps, visit ShopMartingale.com/HowtoQuilt for free downloadable information.

1. Layer the quilt top with batting and backing; baste the layers together.

2. Quilt by hand or machine. The quilt shown is machine quilted with an allover meander pattern.

3. Make double-fold binding using the black solid 2"-wide strips. Attach the binding to the quilt.

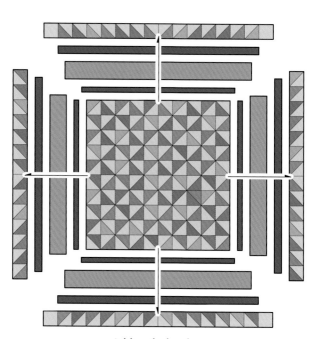

Adding the borders

My, Oh Pie!

An antique pie safe was typically used to protect pies and other perishables from outside elements (think insects, animals, and inquisitive little children). Today, if you're fortunate enough to own one, it's more likely to store books, antique linens, or favorite crockery. Sew yourself an easy-as-pie eight-block runner that will look great on your family dinner table.

FINISHED TABLE RUNNER: 25¾" × 39¾" | FINISHED BLOCK: 5" × 5"

Designed by Paula Barnes; pieced by Mary Ellen Robison; quilted by Cathy Peters and Lynn Graham

MATERIALS

Yardage is based on 42"-wide fabric.

- ⅝ yard of light print for blocks and inner border
- ¼ yard of medium brown print for blocks
- ¼ yard of dark brown print for blocks
- ½ yard of light blue print for setting squares, setting triangles, and corner triangles
- ⅞ yard of dark blue print for outer border and binding
- 1¼ yards of fabric for backing
- 30" × 44" piece of batting
- 1" finished Star Singles papers (optional)*

*See "Using Star Singles" on page 41 before cutting fabrics.

CUTTING

All measurements include ¼" seam allowances.

From the light print, cut:
4 strips, 2¼" × 42"; crosscut into 64 squares, 2¼" × 2¼"
5 strips, 1½" × 42"; crosscut *3 of the strips* into:
    2 strips, 1½" × 28¾"
    2 strips, 1½" × 16¾"
    8 squares, 1½" × 1½"

From the medium brown print, cut:
3 strips, 2¼" × 42"; crosscut into 48 squares, 2¼" × 2¼"

From the dark brown print, cut:
1 strip, 2¼" × 42"; crosscut into 16 squares, 2¼" × 2¼"
2 strips, 1½" × 42"

Continued on page 41

Continued from page 39

From the light blue print, cut:

2 squares, 8⅜" × 8⅜"; cut into quarters diagonally
    to yield 8 setting triangles

3 squares, 5½" × 5½"

2 squares, 4½" × 4½"; cut in half diagonally to yield
    4 corner triangles

From the dark blue print, cut:

4 strips, 5" × 42"; crosscut into:
    2 strips, 5" × 30¾"
    2 strips, 5" × 25¾"

4 strips, 2" × 42"

♦ *Using Star Singles*

If you use the 1" Star Singles papers, *do not* cut the 2¼" squares from the light, medium brown, and dark brown prints. Instead, cut the pieces listed below. Then skip steps 1 and 2 of "Making the Blocks" below and follow the package instructions to piece 96 medium brown and 32 dark brown half-square-triangle units.

From the light print, cut:
16 squares, 4½" × 4½"

From the medium brown print, cut:
12 squares, 4½" × 4½"

From the dark brown print, cut:
4 squares, 4½" × 4½"

MAKING THE BLOCKS

Press the seam allowances as indicated by the arrows in the illustrations.

1. Referring to "Half-Square-Triangle Units" on page 78, mark the light 2¼" squares. Layer 48 of the marked squares right sides together with the medium brown 2¼" squares. Sew, cut, and press; then trim the units to 1½" square. Make 96 medium brown half-square-triangle units.

Make 96 units.

2. Using the 16 remaining marked light squares, repeat step 1 using dark brown 2¼" squares to make 32 dark brown half-square-triangle units.

Make 32 units.

3. Lay out three medium brown units from step 1 and one dark brown unit from step 2 in two rows as shown. Sew together the units in each row. Join the rows to make a corner unit that measures 2½" square, including seam allowances. Make 32 corner units.

Make 32 units,
2½" × 2½".

4. Sew together one light 1½" × 42" strip and one dark brown 1½" × 42" strip. Make two strip sets. Cut into 32 segments that measure 1½" wide.

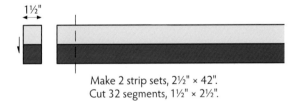

Make 2 strip sets, 2½" × 42".
Cut 32 segments, 1½" × 2½".

5. Arrange four corner units from step 3, four segments from step 4, and one light 1½" square in three rows as shown on page 42. Sew the units into rows and then sew the rows together to complete the block. Make eight Single Wedding Ring blocks that measure 5½" square, including seam allowances.

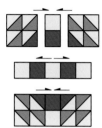

Make 8 blocks,
5½" × 5½".

ASSEMBLING THE TABLE-RUNNER TOP

1. Arrange and sew the blocks and light blue setting squares together in diagonal rows, adding the light blue setting triangles to the ends of each row as indicated. Join the rows, adding the light blue corner triangles last. The table-runner top should measure approximately 14¾" × 28¾", including seam allowances.

Runner assembly

2. Sew the light 1½" × 28¾" strips to the long edges of the runner. Sew the light 1½" × 16¾" strips to the short edges. The runner top should measure 16¾" × 30¾", including seam allowances.

3. Sew the dark blue 5" × 30¾" strips to the long edges of the runner. Sew the dark blue 5" × 25¾" strips to the short edges to complete the runner, which should measure 25¾" × 39¾".

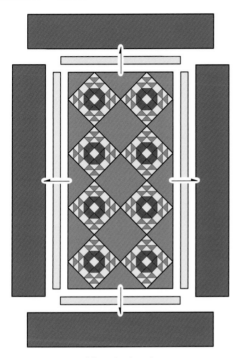

Adding the borders

FINISHING THE TABLE RUNNER

For more details on any finishing steps, visit ShopMartingale.com/HowtoQuilt for free downloadable information.

1. Layer the runner with batting and backing; baste the layers together.

2. Quilt by hand or machine. The runner shown is machine quilted with fleur-de-lis motifs in the blocks and a double pumpkin seed design in the border.

3. Make double-fold binding using the dark blue 2"-wide strips. Attach the binding to the runner.

Scraps Made Simple

Write it down. *I'll save my scraps and put them to good use! I promise!* Then get ready to put your promise into action with a quilt that's tailor-made for scrap lovers. It's as easy as making a half-square triangle. What elevates the ordinary into extraordinary is the diversity of prints, colors, and backgrounds you pull together. Even the borders are scrappy!

FINISHED QUILT: 28½" × 28½" | **FINISHED BLOCK: 6" × 6"**

MATERIALS

Yardage is based on 42"-wide fabric. Fat eighths are 9" × 21".

- 6" × 17" piece *each* of 7 assorted light prints for blocks and border corners
- 6" × 12" piece *each* of 10 assorted dark red and brown prints for blocks and border corners (referred to collectively as "dark")
- ¼ yard of tan print for sashing
- ⅛ yard *each* of 4 assorted brown prints for border
- ¼ yard of dark brown print for binding
- 1 yard of fabric for backing
- 33" × 33" piece of batting
- 1½" finished Star Singles papers (optional)*

See "Using Star Singles" on page 46 before cutting fabrics.

CUTTING

All measurements include ¼" seam allowances.

From *each* of the 7 light prints, cut:
12 squares, 2¾" × 2¾" (84 total; 4 will be extra)

From *each* of the 10 dark prints, cut:
8 squares, 2¾" × 2¾" (80 total)

From the tan print, cut:
5 strips, 1½" × 42"; crosscut into:
    4 strips, 1½" × 22½"
    12 strips, 1½" × 6½"

From *each* of the 4 brown prints, cut:
1 strip, 3½" × 22½" (4 total)

From the dark brown print, cut:
4 strips, 2" × 42"

◆ Using Star Singles

If you use the 1½" Star Singles papers, *do not* cut the 2¾" squares from the light and dark prints. Instead, cut the pieces listed below. Then skip step 1 of "Making the Blocks" below and follow the package instructions to piece 160 light/dark half-square-triangle units.

From *each* of the light prints, cut:
3 squares, 5½" × 5½" (21 total; 1 will be extra)

From *each* of the dark prints, cut:
2 squares, 5½" × 5½" (20 total)

MAKING THE BLOCKS

Press the seam allowances as indicated by the arrows in the illustrations.

1. Referring to "Half-Square-Triangle Units" on page 78, mark the light 2¾" squares and layer them right sides together with the dark 2¾" squares. Sew, cut, and press; then trim the units to 2" square. Make 160 half-square-triangle units.

Make 160 units.

2. Lay out 16 assorted triangle units in four rows of four, orienting the units as shown. Sew the units into rows. Join the rows to make a block measuring 6½" square, including seam allowances. Make nine blocks. The remaining half-square-triangle units are for the border.

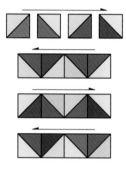 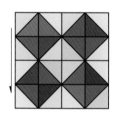

Make 9 blocks,
6½" × 6½".

ASSEMBLING THE QUILT TOP

1. Sew together four tan 1½" × 6½" sashing strips and three blocks to make a block row. Make three rows measuring 6½" × 22½", including seam allowances.

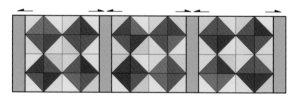

Make 3 rows,
6½" × 22½".

2. Join the tan 1½" × 22½" sashing strips and block rows as shown in the quilt assembly diagram on page 48. The quilt top should measure 22½" square.

Designed by Paula Barnes; pieced by Mary Ellen Robison; quilted by Cathy Peters and Lynn Graham

ADDING THE BORDER

1. Lay out four of the remaining half-square-triangle units in two rows of two, orienting the units as shown. Sew the units into rows. Join the rows to make a border block measuring 3½" square, including seam allowances. Make four border blocks.

Make 4 blocks,
3½" × 3½".

2. Sew brown 3½" × 22½" strips to the sides of the quilt. Join a border block to each end of the remaining strips. Sew these strips to the top and bottom of the quilt to complete the quilt top, which should measure 28½" square.

FINISHING THE QUILT

For more details on any finishing steps, visit ShopMartingale.com/HowtoQuilt for free downloadable information.

1. Layer the quilt top with batting and backing; baste the layers together.

2. Quilt by hand or machine. The quilt shown is machine quilted with a feathered flower in each block of the quilt center and stitched in the ditch of the sashing pieces. Each border block is stitched with a fleur-de-lis design made of feathers and the border strips are stitched with feathered vines.

3. Make double-fold binding using the dark brown 2"-wide strips. Attach the binding to the quilt.

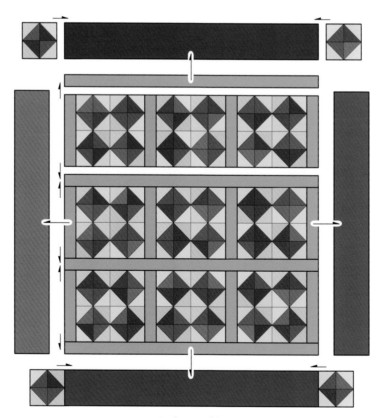

Quilt assembly

Picture This

We're spoiled by technology. Who'd have guessed we would carry a calculator, computer, and camera in our pocket every day? Not us. But we do take advantage of the tools. One trick is to choose fabrics based on the border or busiest print in the quilt. And if we're unsure of the color value of the mix, we'll shoot a black-and-white photo to make sure the balance looks good. Try it!

FINISHED QUILT: 28½" × 28½" | FINISHED BLOCK: 6" × 6"

MATERIALS

Yardage is based on 42"-wide fabric.

- 6" × 17" piece *each* of 7 assorted light prints for blocks and border corners
- 6" × 12" piece *each* of 10 assorted black, tan, and gray prints for blocks and border corners (referred to collectively as "dark")
- ¼ yard of black print for sashing
- ½ yard of tan floral for border
- ¼ yard of black solid for binding
- 1 yard of fabric for backing
- 33" × 33" piece of batting
- 1½" finished Star Singles papers (optional)*

*See "Using Star Singles" on page 51 before cutting fabrics.

CUTTING

All measurements include ¼" seam allowances.

From *each* of the light prints, cut:
12 squares, 2¾" × 2¾" (84 total; 4 will be extra)

From *each* of the dark prints, cut:
8 squares, 2¾" × 2¾" (80 total)

From the black print, cut:
5 strips, 1½" × 42"; crosscut into:
    4 strips, 1½" × 22½"
    12 strips, 1½" × 6½"

From the tan floral, cut:
4 strips, 3½" × 22½"

From the black solid, cut:
4 strips, 2" × 42"

◆ *Using Star Singles*

If you use the 1½" Star Singles papers, *do not* cut the 2¾" squares from the light and dark prints. Instead, cut the pieces listed below. Then skip step 1 of "Making the Blocks" below and follow the package instructions to piece 160 light/dark half-square-triangle units.

From *each* of the light prints, cut:

3 squares, 5½" × 5½" (21 total; 1 will be extra)

From *each* of the dark prints, cut:

2 squares, 5½" × 5½" (20 total)

MAKING THE BLOCKS

Press the seam allowances as indicated by the arrows in the illustrations.

1. Referring to "Half-Square-Triangle Units" on page 78, mark the light 2¾" squares and layer them right sides together with the dark 2¾" squares. Sew, cut, and press; then trim the units to 2" square. Make 160 half-square-triangle units.

Make 160 units.

2. Lay out 16 assorted half-square-triangle units in four rows of four, orienting the units as shown. Sew the units into rows. Join the rows to make a Star block measuring

6½" square, including seam allowances. Make nine blocks. Set aside the remaining units for the border.

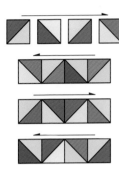 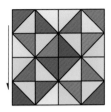

Make 9 blocks,
6½" × 6½".

ASSEMBLING THE QUILT TOP

1. Sew together four black print 1½" × 6½" sashing strips and three blocks to make a block row. Make three rows measuring 6½" × 22½", including seam allowances.

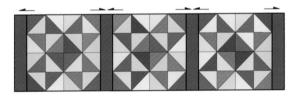

Make 3 rows, 6½" × 22½".

2. Join the black print 1½" × 22½" sashing strips and block rows, alternating them as shown in the quilt assembly diagram on page 53. The quilt top should measure 22½" square, including seam allowances.

ADDING THE BORDER

1. Lay out four remaining half-square-triangle units in two rows of two, orienting the units as shown. Sew the units into rows. Join the rows to make a border block measuring 3½" square, including seam allowances. Make four border blocks.

Make 4 blocks,
3½" × 3½".

Designed by Paula Barnes; pieced by Mary Ellen Robison; quilted by Pat Meeks

2. Sew tan floral 3½" × 22½" strips to the sides of the quilt. Sew a border block to each end of the remaining tan floral 3½" × 22½" strips. Sew these strips to the top and bottom of the quilt. The quilt top should measure 28½" square.

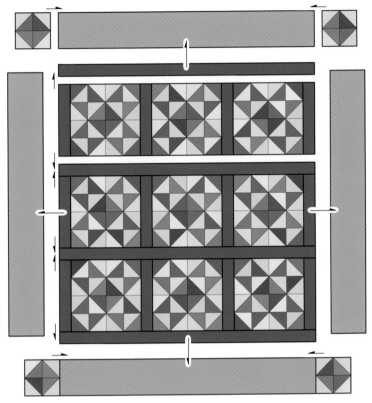

Quilt assembly

FINISHING THE QUILT

For more details on any finishing steps, visit ShopMartingale.com/HowtoQuilt for free downloadable information.

1. Layer the quilt top with batting and backing; baste the layers together.

2. Quilt by hand or machine. The quilt shown is machine quilted with an allover meander design.

3. Make double-fold binding using the black solid 2"-wide strips. Attach the binding to the quilt.

Four Square

Do you recall playing the game Four Square as a youngster? (It's thought the game originated as Boxball around the time of World War I.) A rubber ball was bounced between players who had to hit the ball into another player's square without the ball bouncing more than once. There are fewer "rules" to read up on to make this four-square cutie, but we promise, it's just as fun.

FINISHED QUILT: 24½" × 24½" | FINISHED BLOCK: 6" × 6"

*Designed by Paula Barnes; pieced by
Mary Ellen Robison; quilted by Pat Meeks*

MATERIALS

Yardage is based on 42"-wide fabric.

- ⅛ yard of red print for blocks
- ⅝ yard of brown print for blocks, sashing, outer border corners, and binding
- ⅛ yard of gold print for blocks and sashing squares
- ¼ yard of beige print for blocks and inner border
- ¼ yard of red stripe for outer border
- ⅞ yard of fabric for backing
- 29" × 29" piece of batting

CUTTING

All measurements include ¼" seam allowances.

From the red print, cut:
2 strips, 1½" × 42"; crosscut into 48 squares, 1½" × 1½"

From the brown print, cut:
1 strip, 3½" × 42"; crosscut into 4 squares, 3½" × 3½"
5 strips, 2" × 42"; crosscut *2 of the strips* into 12 strips, 2" × 6½"
2 strips, 1½" × 42"; crosscut into 16 pieces, 1½" × 2½"

From the gold print, cut:
1 strip, 2½" × 42"; crosscut into:
    4 squares, 2½" × 2½"
    9 squares, 2" × 2"

From the beige print, cut:
3 strips, 1½" × 42"; crosscut into:
    16 pieces, 1½" × 4½"
    16 squares, 1½" × 1½"
2 strips, 1¼" × 42"; crosscut into:
    2 strips, 1¼" × 18½"
    2 strips, 1¼" × 17"

From the red stripe, cut:
2 strips, 3½" × 42"; crosscut into 4 strips, 3½" × 18½"

Making the Blocks

Press the seam allowances as indicated by the arrows in the illustrations.

1. Arrange and sew four red print 1½" squares, four brown 1½" × 2½" pieces, and one gold 2½" square together in rows as shown. Sew the rows together to make a block center that measures 4½" square, including seam allowances. Make a total of four block centers.

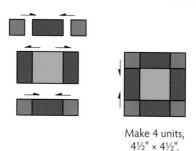

Make 4 units,
4½" × 4½".

2. Draw a diagonal line from corner to corner on the wrong side of the remaining red print 1½" squares. Place a marked square on each end of a beige 1½" × 4½" piece, right sides together. Sew on the marked lines. Trim the excess corner fabric ¼" from the stitched line. Make 16 units, each 1½" × 4½", including seam allowances.

Make 16 units,
1½" × 4½".

◆ Starching Small Pieces

While we always recommend spray starching your fabric *before* cutting, we find it particularly beneficial when working with small pieces. It cuts down on fraying and stretching and also makes for crisper pressing.

3. Arrange and sew four beige 1½" squares, four units from step 2, and one block center together in rows as shown. Join the rows to make a block measuring 6½" square, including seam allowances. Make four blocks total.

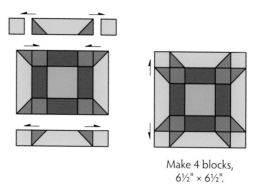

Make 4 blocks,
6½" × 6½".

Assembling the Quilt Top

1. Arrange the gold 2" sashing squares, brown 2" × 6½" sashing strips, and blocks into rows as shown. Join the sashing strips and squares together to create three sashing rows. Sew the blocks and sashing into two block rows. Join the rows to make the quilt center, which should measure 17" square, including seam allowances.

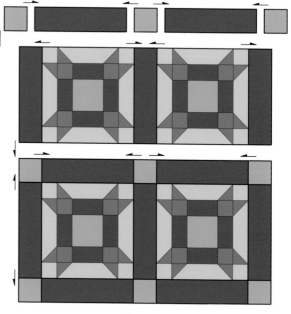

Quilt assembly

2. Sew the beige 1¼" × 17" strips to the sides of the quilt. Sew the beige 1¼" × 18½" strips to the top and bottom. The quilt top should measure 18½" square, including seam allowances.

3. Sew red stripe 3½" × 18½" strips to opposite sides of the quilt top. Sew a brown 3½" square to each end of the remaining red stripe 3½" × 18½" strips. Sew the strips to the top and bottom of the quilt top, which should measure 24½" square.

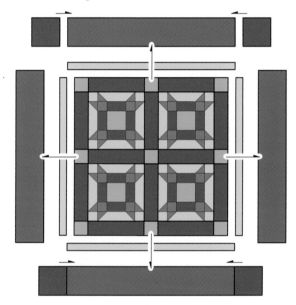

Adding the borders

Finishing the Quilt

For more details on any finishing steps, visit ShopMartingale.com/HowtoQuilt for free downloadable information.

1. Layer the quilt top with batting and backing; baste the layers together.

2. Quilt by hand or machine. The quilt shown is machine quilted with an allover meander design.

3. Make double-fold binding using the remaining brown print 2"-wide strips. Attach the binding to the quilt.

Perk Me Up

If you're like us, quilts are a part of your everyday decor. We love quilts over a ladder, across the foot of a bed, tucked into a little vignette, and hanging on the walls. But the ones we change out most often are tabletop size. Small square quilts are the perfect toppers to swap with the seasons, for special occasions, or to perk up the look of a room. Whatever your reason, go for it!

FINISHED QUILT: 28" × 28" | **FINISHED BLOCK: 5" × 5"**

MATERIALS

Yardage is based on 42"-wide fabric.

- ¼ yard of cream print for blocks
- ¼ yard of ecru print for blocks, sashing squares, and border corner blocks
- ½ yard of blue print for blocks, setting triangles, corner triangles, and border corner blocks
- ¼ yard of golden brown print for blocks and sashing
- ¾ yard of gray floral for border, border corner blocks, and binding
- 1 yard of fabric for backing
- 32" × 32" piece of batting

CUTTING

All measurements include ¼" seam allowances.

From the cream print, cut:
3 strips, 1½" × 42"; crosscut *2 of the strips* into 20 pieces, 1½" × 2½"

From the ecru print, cut:
3 strips, 1½" × 42"; crosscut *2 of the strips* into:
    2 strips, 1½" × 13"
    12 squares, 1½" × 1½"

From the blue print, cut:
1 strip, 9¾" × 42"; crosscut into:
    1 square, 9¾" × 9¾"; cut into quarters diagonally to yield 4 setting triangles
    2 squares, 6" × 6"; cut in half diagonally to yield 4 corner triangles
1 strip, 3" × 42"; crosscut into:
    1 strip, 3" × 13"
    8 pieces, 1½" × 3"
2 strips, 1½" × 42"

From the golden brown print, cut:
3 strips, 1½" × 42"; crosscut into:
    16 strips, 1½" × 5½"
    5 squares, 1½" × 1½"

From the gray floral, cut:
2 strips, 5" × 42"; crosscut into 4 strips, 5" × 19"
1 strip, 3" × 42"; crosscut into 4 squares, 3" × 3"
4 strips, 2" × 42"

MAKING THE BLOCKS

Press the seam allowances as indicated by the arrows in the illustrations.

1. Sew together a cream and a blue 1½" × 42" strip to make a strip set. Cut the strip set into 20 cream/blue segments, 1½" wide.

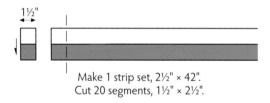

Make 1 strip set, 2½" × 42".
Cut 20 segments, 1½" × 2½".

2. Repeat step 1 using a ecru and a blue 1½" × 42" strip. Make 20 ecru/blue segments, 1½" wide.

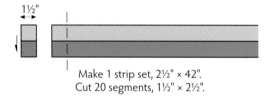

Make 1 strip set, 2½" × 42".
Cut 20 segments, 1½" × 2½".

3. Sew a cream 1½" × 2½" piece to the left side of a segment from step 1 to make a corner unit. Make 10. Adding the cream 1½" × 2½" piece to the right side of the segment instead, make 10 reversed corner units. Each unit should measure 2½" square, including seam allowances.

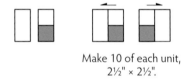

Make 10 of each unit,
2½" × 2½".

4. Arrange two corner units and two reversed corner units from step 3, four segments from step 2, and one golden brown 1½" square in three rows as shown. Sew the units into rows and then sew the rows together to complete the block. Make five blocks that measure 5½" square, including seam allowances.

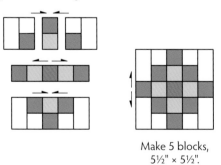

Make 5 blocks,
5½" × 5½".

ASSEMBLING THE QUILT TOP

1. Referring to the quilt assembly diagram below, arrange the blocks, golden brown 1½" × 5½" sashing strips, ecru 1½" sashing squares, and blue setting triangles in diagonal rows. First join the sashing squares and strips in each sashing row. Then join the pieces in each block row.

2. Sew the short sashing rows to the adjacent block rows, then add the blue setting triangles to the ends of each short block row as indicated. Join all remaining diagonal rows, then add the blue corner triangles last to complete the quilt center, which should be approximately 19" square, including seam allowances.

ADDING THE BORDER

1. Sew together a blue 3" × 13" strip and two ecru 1½" × 13" strips to make a strip set. Cut the strip set into eight segments, 1½" wide.

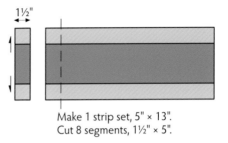

1½"

Make 1 strip set, 5" × 13".
Cut 8 segments, 1½" × 5".

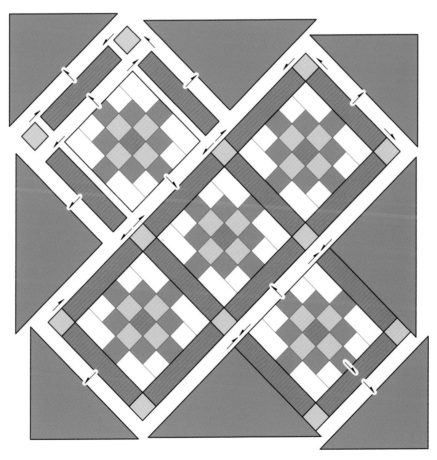

Quilt assembly

Designed by Paula Barnes; pieced by Mary Ellen Robison; quilted by Cathy Peters and Lynn Graham

2. Sew blue 1½" × 3" pieces to opposite edges of a gray floral 3" square. Add segments from step 1 on page 61 to the top and bottom edges to make a border corner block. The block should measure 5" square, including seam allowances. Make four blocks.

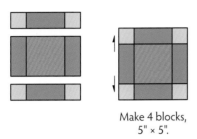

Make 4 blocks,
5" × 5".

3. Sew gray floral 5" × 19" strips to opposite sides of the quilt center. Add a corner block to each end of the remaining gray floral 5" × 19" strips. Sew these strips to the top and bottom edges of the quilt to complete the quilt top. The quilt top should measure 28" square.

FINISHING THE QUILT

For more details on any finishing steps, visit ShopMartingale.com/HowtoQuilt for free downloadable information.

1. Layer the quilt top with batting and backing; baste the layers together.

2. Quilt by hand or machine. The quilt shown is machine quilted with an echoing flower design in each block, bunches of leaves in each setting and corner triangle, and arcing lines in the border.

3. Make double-fold binding using the gray floral 2"-wide strips. Attach the binding to the quilt.

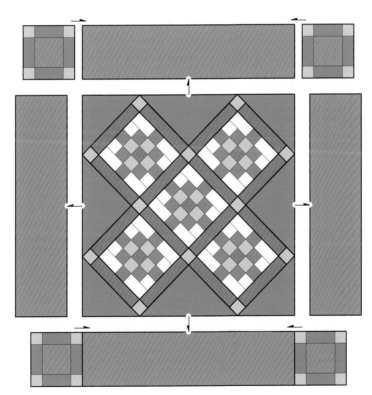

Adding the border

Striking Stars

Drama. We may not love it in all aspects of our lives, but we do love it in our quilts. And nothing sets the stage for drama like solid black. A rainbow of star blocks shines bright, each star twinkling in its own mix of prints and hues, like an artist's painting against an all-black canvas. Contrast between small and large stars adds a second layer of eye-catching, breathtaking depth.

FINISHED QUILT: 26" × 26" | FINISHED BLOCK: 6" × 6"

Designed by Paula Barnes; pieced by Mary Ellen Robison; quilted by Pat Meeks

MATERIALS

Yardage is based on 42"-wide fabric.

- 2½" × 42" strip *each* of 13 assorted dark prints for blocks
- ½ yard of light print for blocks
- ⅝ yard of black solid for blocks, setting triangles, corner triangles, and binding
- ⅞ yard of fabric for backing
- 30" × 30" piece of batting

CUTTING

All measurements include ¼" seam allowances.

From *each* of the dark prints, cut:

1 strip, 1½" × 42"; crosscut into:
    4 pieces, 1½" × 4½" (52 total)
    12 squares, 1½" × 1½" (156 total)

From the light print, cut:

10 strips, 1½" × 42"; crosscut into:
    52 pieces, 1½" × 2½"
    156 squares, 1½" × 1½"

From the black solid, cut:

1 strip, 9¾" × 42"; crosscut into:
    2 squares, 9¾" × 9¾"; cut into quarters diagonally
        to yield 8 setting triangles
    2 squares, 5⅛" × 5⅛"; cut in half diagonally to yield
        4 corner triangles
1 strip, 2½" × 42"; crosscut into 13 squares, 2½" × 2½"
3 strips, 2" × 42"

MAKING THE BLOCKS

Press the seam allowances as indicated by the arrows in the illustrations.

1. Gather eight matching dark print 1½" squares. Draw a diagonal line from corner to corner on the wrong side of the dark squares. Place a marked square on one end of a light 1½" × 2½" piece, right sides together. Sew on the

marked line. Trim the excess corner fabric ¼" from the stitched line. Place a marked square on the opposite end of the light piece. Sew and trim as before to make a flying-geese unit measuring 1½" × 2½", including seam allowances. Make four matching units. Repeat to make a set of four matching units from each of the 13 dark prints (52 total).

Make 13 sets of 4 units,
1½" × 2½".

2. Arrange and sew four light 1½" squares, four matching units from step 1, and one black 2½" square together in three rows as shown. Join the rows to make a block center measuring 4½" square, including seam allowances. Make 13 block centers total.

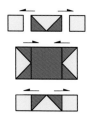

Make 13 block centers,
4½" × 4½".

3. For one block, gather four 1½" squares and four 1½" × 4½" pieces from one dark print and eight light 1½" squares. Draw a diagonal line from corner to corner on the wrong side of the light 1½" squares. Place a marked square on each end of a dark 1½" × 4½" piece, right sides together. Sew on the marked lines. Trim the excess corner fabric ¼" from the stitched line. Make four matching units, each 1½" × 4½", including seam allowances.

 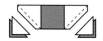

Make 4 units,
1½" × 4½".

4. Lay out the units from step 3, the matching 1½" squares, and a block center that uses a different print in three rows as shown. Sew the pieces together in rows, and then join the rows to make a block that measures 6½" square, including seam allowances. Repeat to make 13 blocks total.

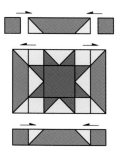
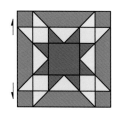

Make 13 blocks,
6½" × 6½".

ASSEMBLING THE QUILT TOP

Referring to the quilt assembly diagram below, arrange and sew the blocks together in diagonal rows, adding the black setting triangles to the ends of each row as indicated. Join the rows, adding the black corner triangles last. The quilt top should be approximately 26" square.

FINISHING THE QUILT

For more details on any finishing steps, visit ShopMartingale.com/HowtoQuilt for free downloadable information.

1. Layer the quilt top with batting and backing; baste the layers together.

2. Quilt by hand or machine. The quilt shown is machine quilted with an allover meander design.

3. Make double-fold binding using the black solid 2"-wide strips. Attach the binding to the quilt.

Quilt assembly

Hill Country Heritage

Texas Hill Country is known for its changing landscape, mix of city and rural life, dozens of wineries and vineyards, and pretty-as-a-picture vistas. Located in the crossroads between West, Central, and South Texas, it's a trip worth taking. Also worth taking? A tip for using Star Singles to make the triangle squares for this mini. They're a time-saver and accuracy maker!

FINISHED QUILT: 30½" × 30½" | FINISHED BLOCK: 4" × 4"

*Designed by Paula Barnes; pieced by
Mary Ellen Robison; quilted by Pat Meeks*

MATERIALS

Yardage is based on 42"-wide fabric. Fat quarters are 18" × 21".

- 4 fat quarters of assorted light prints for blocks
- 4 fat quarters of assorted red prints for blocks
- 3 fat quarters of assorted navy prints for blocks
- ¼ yard of brown print for inner border
- ⅞ yard of navy print for outer border and binding
- 1 yard of fabric for backing
- 35" × 35" piece of batting
- 1" and 2" finished Star Singles papers (optional)*

*See "Using Star Singles" on page 70 before cutting fabrics.

CUTTING

All measurements include ¼" seam allowances.

From *each* of the light prints, cut:
2 strips, 3¼" × 21"; crosscut into 8 squares, 3¼" × 3¼"
 (32 total; 4 will be extra)
3 strips, 2¼" × 21"; crosscut into 24 squares, 2¼" × 2¼"
 (96 total)

From *each* of the red prints, cut:
1 strip, 3¼" × 21"; crosscut into 4 squares, 3¼" × 3¼"
 (16 total)
2 strips, 2¼" × 21"; crosscut into 12 squares, 2¼" × 2¼"
 (48 total)

From *each* of the navy fat quarters, cut:
1 strip, 3¼" × 21"; crosscut into 4 squares, 3¼" × 3¼"
 (12 total)
2 strips, 2¼" × 21"; crosscut into 16 squares, 2¼" × 2¼"
 (48 total)

Continued on page 70

Continued from page 69

From the brown print, cut:

4 strips, 1½" × 42"; crosscut into:

    2 strips, 1½" × 22½"

    2 strips, 1½" × 20½"

From the navy print, cut:

4 strips, 4½" × 42"; crosscut into:

    2 strips, 4½" × 30½"

    2 strips, 4½" × 22½"

4 strips, 2" × 42"

◆ *Using Star Singles*

If you want to use 1" and 2" finished Star Singles papers, *do not* cut the 2¼" and 3¼" squares from the assorted lights, red prints, and navy prints. Instead, cut the pieces listed below. Then skip steps 1–4 of "Making the Blocks" below, and follow the package instructions to piece 96 red and 96 navy small half-square-triangle units and 32 red and 24 navy large units.

From *each* of the light prints, cut:

2 squares, 6½" × 6½" (8 total; 1 will be extra)

6 squares, 4½" × 4½" (24 total)

From *each* of the red prints, cut:

1 square, 6½" × 6½" (4 total)

3 squares, 4½" × 4½" (12 total)

From *each* of the navy fat quarters, cut:

1 square, 6½" × 6½" (3 total)

4 squares, 4½" × 4½" (12 total)

MAKING THE BLOCKS

Press the seam allowances as indicated by the arrows in the illustrations.

1. Gather a set of four matching light 2¼" squares and four matching red 2¼" squares. Referring to "Half-Square-Triangle Units" on page 78, mark the light 2¼" squares. Layer the marked light squares right sides together with the red squares. Sew, cut, and press; then trim the units to 1½" square. Make eight red small half-square-triangle units. Repeat to make 12 sets of eight matching units (96 total); keep matching sets together.

Make 12 sets of
8 matching units.

2. Gather a set of four matching light 2¼" squares and four matching navy 2¼" squares. Make eight navy small half-square-triangle units. Repeat to make 12 sets of eight matching units (96 total).

Make 12 sets of
8 matching units.

3. Gather a set of two matching light 3¼" squares and two matching red 3¼" squares. Repeat to mark the light 3¼" squares. Layer the marked light squares right sides together with the red squares. Sew, cut, and press; then trim the units to 2½" square. Make four red large half-square-triangle units. Repeat to make eight sets of four matching units (32 total); keep matching sets together.

Make 8 sets of
4 matching units.

4. Gather a set of two matching light 3¼" squares and two matching navy 3¼" squares. Make four navy large half-square-triangle units. Repeat to make six sets of four matching units (24 total); keep matching sets together.

Make 6 sets of
4 matching units.

5. Sew a set of four matching units from step 3 together in two rows as shown. Join the rows to make a red Triangle block. The block should measure 4½" square, including seam allowances. Make seven red Triangle blocks (you'll have four red large half-square-triangle units left over).

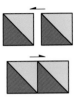

Make 7 blocks,
4½" × 4½".

6. Repeat step 5 using four matching units from step 4 to make a navy Triangle block. Make six Triangle blocks.

Make 6 blocks,
4½" × 4½".

7. Gather a set of eight matching units from step 1 and eight matching units from step 2. Lay out the units in four rows as shown, noting the color placement and triangle rotation. Sew the pieces together in rows, then join the rows to make a Mosaic block. Make 12 blocks, each 4½" square, including seam allowances.

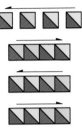

Make 12 blocks,
4½" × 4½".

ASSEMBLING THE QUILT TOP

1. Arrange the blocks into five rows of five blocks each, alternating the blocks as shown. Sew the blocks into rows and then sew the rows together. The quilt center should measure 20½" square, including seam allowances.

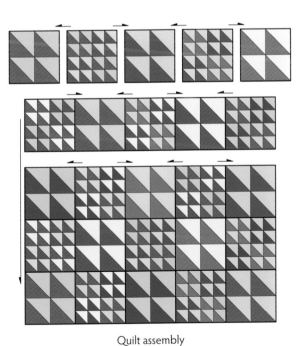

Quilt assembly

2. Sew the brown 1½" × 20½" strips to the sides of the quilt. Sew the brown 1½" × 22½" strips to the top and bottom. The quilt top should measure 22½" square, including seam allowances.

3. Sew the navy 4½" × 22½" strips to the sides of the quilt. Sew the navy 4½" × 30½" strips to the top and bottom. The quilt top should measure 30½" square.

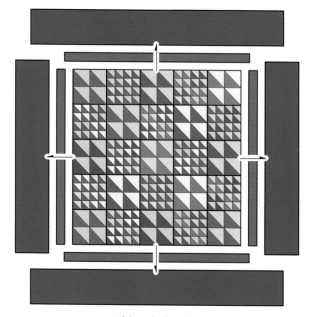

Adding the borders

FINISHING THE QUILT

For more details on any finishing steps, visit ShopMartingale.com/HowtoQuilt for free downloadable information.

1. Layer the quilt top with batting and backing; baste the layers together.

2. Quilt by hand or machine. The quilt shown is machine quilted with an allover meander design.

3. Make double-fold binding using the navy 2"-wide strips. Attach the binding to the quilt.

Crossroads

What appears to be an intricate weaving of lines crossing over and under one another is anything but. Strip piecing and careful color placement while making the blocks yields spectacular results when the quilt comes together. Just nine blocks that are straight set with simple sashing creates a fool-the-eye look you'll love!

FINISHED QUILT: 35½" × 35½" | **FINISHED BLOCK: 8" × 8"**

MATERIALS

Yardage is based on 42"-wide fabric.

- ½ yard of tan print for blocks and sashing
- ⅞ yard of brown print for blocks, border, and binding
- ⅓ yard of navy print A (medium scale) for blocks
- ⅓ yard of navy print B (small scale) for blocks and sashing squares
- ⅓ yard of light print for blocks
- 1⅛ yards of fabric for backing
- 40" × 40" piece of batting

CUTTING

All measurements include ¼" seam allowances.

From the tan print, cut:
9 strips, 1½" × 42"; crosscut into:
    24 strips, 1½" × 8½"
    72 squares, 1½" × 1½"

From the brown print, cut:
4 strips, 4" × 42"; crosscut into:
    2 strips, 4" × 35½"
    2 strips, 4" × 28½"
3 strips, 1½" × 42"; crosscut into 36 pieces, 1½" × 2½"
4 strips, 2" × 42"

From navy print A, cut:
1 strip, 2½" × 42"; crosscut into 9 squares, 2½" × 2½"
5 strips, 1½" × 42"; crosscut *2 of the strips* into 36 squares, 1½" × 1½"

From navy print B, cut:
6 strips, 1½" × 42"; crosscut *1 of the strips* into 16 squares, 1½" × 1½"

From the light print, cut:
8 strips, 1½" × 42"

MAKING THE BLOCKS

Press the seam allowances as indicated by the arrows in the illustrations.

1. Draw a diagonal line from corner to corner on the wrong side of the tan 1½" squares. Place a marked square on one end of a brown 1½" × 2½" piece, right sides together. Sew on the marked line. Trim the excess corner fabric ¼" from the stitched line. Place a marked square on the opposite end of the brown piece. Sew and trim as before to make a flying-geese unit measuring 1½" × 2½", including seam allowances. Make 36 units.

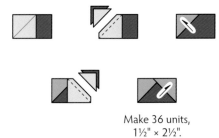

Make 36 units,
1½" × 2½".

2. Arrange and sew four navy A 1½" squares, four flying-geese units from step 1, and one navy A 2½" square together into three rows as shown. Sew the rows together to make a block center that measures 4½" square, including seam allowances. Make a total of nine block centers.

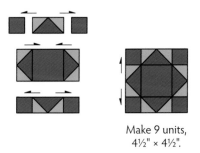

Make 9 units,
4½" × 4½".

3. Sew together a light and a navy B 1½" × 42" strip to make a strip set. Make five strip sets. Cut the strip sets into 36 total segments, 4½" wide.

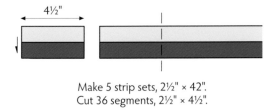

Make 5 strip sets, 2½" × 42".
Cut 36 segments, 2½" × 4½".

4. Sew together a light and a navy A 1½" × 42" strip to make a strip set. Make three strip sets. Cut the strip sets into 72 total segments, 1½" wide.

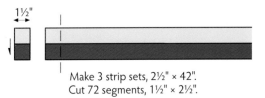

Make 3 strip sets, 2½" × 42".
Cut 72 segments, 1½" × 2½".

5. Sew together two of the segments from step 4 to make a four-patch unit that measures 2½" square, including seam allowances. Make 36 four-patch units.

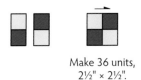

Make 36 units,
2½" × 2½".

6. Arrange four units from step 5, four segments from step 3, and one block center in three rows as shown. Sew the units into rows and then sew the rows together to complete the block. Make nine blocks that measure 8½" square, including seam allowances.

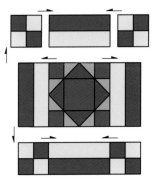

Make 9 blocks, 8½" × 8½".

Designed by Paula Barnes; pieced by Mary Ellen Robison; quilted by Pat Meeks

ASSEMBLING THE QUILT TOP

1. Sew together four navy B 1½" squares and three tan 1½" × 8½" strips in a row. The sashing row should be 1½" × 28½", including seam allowances. Make four sashing rows.

Make 4 sashing rows, 1½" × 28½".

2. Sew together four tan 1½" × 8½" strips and three blocks in a row. The block row should be 8½" × 28½", including seam allowances. Make three block rows.

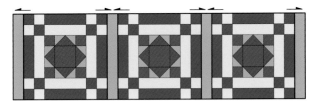

Make 3 block rows, 8½" × 28½".

3. Join the sashing rows and block rows to make the quilt center. The quilt center should measure 28½" square, including seam allowances.

4. Sew the brown 4" × 28½" strips to the left and right edges of the quilt. Sew the brown 4" × 35½" strips to the top and bottom to complete the quilt top. The quilt top should measure 35½" square.

FINISHING THE QUILT

For more details on any finishing steps, visit ShopMartingale.com/HowtoQuilt for free downloadable information.

1. Layer the quilt top with batting and backing; baste the layers together.

2. Quilt by hand or machine. The quilt shown is machine quilted with an allover meander design.

3. Make double-fold binding using the brown 2"-wide strips. Attach the binding to the quilt.

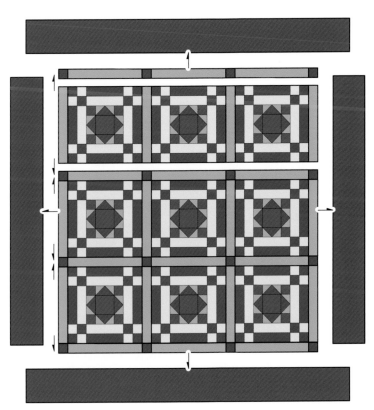

Quilt assembly

Quiltmaking Basics

We all come to quiltmaking with varying skill levels and experiences, but accuracy is the most important qualification needed to successfully complete a quilt.

CUTTING

Let's start with accuracy in cutting.

The instructions for all the projects in this book use rotary cutting, and a standard ¼"-wide seam allowance is included in all measurements. Before you begin cutting, we suggest starching and pressing your fabric well. Put a new blade in your rotary cutter. These are basic steps that go a long way toward successful cutting.

An accurate ¼" seam allowance is essential in quiltmaking. Consider purchasing a ¼" presser foot for your sewing machine. Whether you use a ¼" foot or a standard foot, take the time to test your accuracy before you begin piecing your project. To check accuracy, follow these steps.

1. Cut three 1½" × 4" strips.

2. Sew the strips together. Press the seam allowances toward the outer strips.

3. Using a ruler, measure the width of the center strip. It should measure 1". If your center strip is larger than 1", your seam allowance is too narrow. If your center strip

is smaller than 1", your seam allowance is too wide. Cut new strips and repeat until the center strip measures exactly 1".

You can also use ¼" graph paper to check your seam allowance. Place a piece of graph paper under the presser foot and sew on the first ¼" line. Affix a piece of painter's tape or ¼" quilter's tape along the edge of the paper. Remove the graph paper and sew three strips together using the seam guide, and then check the center strip for accuracy. Once you know the seam guide is in the correct position, build it up with another layer or two of tape.

After sewing seams accurately, pressing becomes the next important step. Recommended pressing directions for seam allowances are included throughout the project illustrations. Remember, you are pressing to set seams, not ironing the wrinkles out of a shirt.

HALF-SQUARE-TRIANGLE UNITS

We love half-square-triangle units, as you can see from our quilts! They add so much to a simple block. There are many different methods and tools available for making them, and you may already have a favorite technique. If so, feel free to use it. For these projects, we've generally used the technique of piecing the units from layered squares, without cutting triangles first.

We've also provided cutting options for the projects in which purchased triangle papers would be a good option. We like the ease and accuracy of Star Singles papers, designed by Liz Eagan of Spinning Star Design, and we often use them in our quiltmaking. They make several identical half-square-triangle units at a time. Star Singles are widely available at quilt shops and online.

When making half-square-triangle units without the papers, we cut squares oversized and trim the final units after pressing. This guarantees complete accuracy. In the steps that follow, we've used 1" finished half-square-triangle units as an example.

1. Cut a light and a dark square, 1¼" larger than the desired finished size. In this case, cut the squares 2¼" × 2¼".

2. With a pencil or fabric marker and ruler, draw a diagonal line from corner to corner on the wrong side of the lighter 2¼" square.

3. Place the marked square on the dark 2¼" square with right sides together. Align the raw edges and sew ¼" from both sides of the marked line.

Mark diagonal.   Sew ¼" from each
                                   side of the line.

4. Cut on the marked line. You'll have two identical half-square-triangle units. Press the seam allowances toward the darker triangle.

Cut on marked line.   Press.

5. Using a square ruler, trim the units to 1½" square, aligning the 45° line of your ruler with the seam. Make sure that the unit under the ruler extends beyond the 1½" mark and trim the right and top edges with your rotary cutter. Rotate the unit 180°, align the newly cut edges with the 1½" marks, and trim the right and top edges.

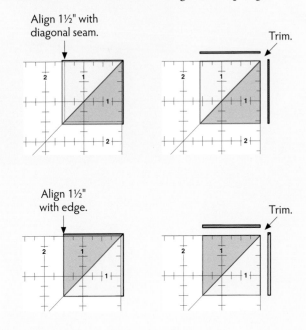

Align 1½" with diagonal seam.   Trim.

Align 1½" with edge.   Trim.

QUILTING

Your top is complete, so now it's time to prepare it for quilting. For many of us, that means making a backing and passing the project on to a machine quilter. The pattern instructions provide our yardage recommendations for the backing. Most of the quilts in this book are small enough so that you won't have to piece the backing— unless you want to! The instructions allow for at least 2" to 3" extra on each side of the quilt, or a backing that's 4" to 6" larger than the finished quilt dimensions.

BINDING

We most often use a double-fold, straight-grain binding on our quilts, but we cut our strips 2" wide, which is slightly narrower than what is often suggested. We find this width provides a nice, tight binding. Each project indicates the number of binding strips to cut, and the yardage is enough that you can cut 2½"-wide strips if you prefer, either across the fabric width or on the bias.

We have learned that binding cut on the lengthwise grain is not recommended. Crossgrain strips have more flexibility and stretch, ensuring that your quilt will lie flat when bound. Sew the strips end to end to make the continuous binding you will need.

About the Authors

Paula Barnes (right) and **Mary Ellen Robison** (left) met more than 20 years ago when they both moved to the same street in Katy, Texas. Paula taught quilting classes at the local quilt shop, and Mary Ellen was the devoted student. They quickly formed a friendship that went beyond their love of quilting and reproduction fabric to become Red Crinoline Quilts. Although they met in Texas, each one comes from a different part of the country. Mary Ellen was born and raised in New York, while Paula is from Georgia. Theirs is a true North-South friendship.

Mary Ellen and her husband, Peter, live in St. Petersburg, Florida, where she divides her time between sewing quilts for Red Crinoline Quilts, cruising, and traveling to see her three children and their families—Megan, son-in-law Brian, and grandson Adam in Louisville, Kentucky; Brett, daughter-in-law Meredith, and granddaughters Sydney and Julianne in Ballston Lake, New York; and Caitlin in Tampa, Florida.

Paula lives in the Dallas area and is mom to three grown daughters, Alison, Ashley, and Amy; mother-in-law to three sons-in-law, David, Robert, and Alex; and grandmother (or MiMi) to granddaughters Sophie and Ava and grandsons John and Walker. Paula began teaching quilting in 1989 in Dallas, and now travels throughout the United States, teaching and lecturing at quilt guilds and local quilt shops.

You can contact both Mary Ellen and Paula at
Red Crinoline Quilts: info@redcrinolinequilts.com.